A REPORT CARD

THE STATE OF EDUCATION IN INDIA

ANURAG YADAV

Made with ♥ on the Notion Press Platform
www.notionpress.com

Contents

Contents

Foreword

It is my pleasure to write the foreword for "A Report Card" - an in-depth examination of the Indian education system. The authors of this book have done an outstanding job in providing a comprehensive analysis of the state of education in India. From the historical background to the current challenges and solutions, this book offers a wealth of information and insights on the Indian education system.

The authors have also highlighted the impact of the private sector and the global best practices that can be implemented in India, they have also compared Indian education system with that of other countries such as American, UK, Australian and German Education Systems. This provides a unique perspective on the Indian education system and its position in the global context.

Furthermore, the authors have done a commendable job in gathering data and information from a variety of sources, including government documents and reports, educational research studies, and interviews with education experts. This has enabled them to provide a comprehensive overview of the Indian education system and its various components.

I believe that this book will serve as a valuable resource for anyone interested in understanding the Indian education system, its challenges, and its potential for improvement. The insights and recommendations provided in this book will be of great use to educators, policymakers, students, parents, researchers, and anyone interested in ensuring that every child in India receives a quality education.

I highly recommend "A Report Card" to anyone interested in the Indian education system and I am confident that it will be of great value to anyone who reads it. It is an in-depth and comprehensive examination of the Indian education system and an essential read for all those interested in the future of education in India.

Preface

An in-depth analysis of the Indian educational system is provided in "A Report Card." In this book, we explore the historical context of education in India, the state of literacy and enrollment rates today, access and achievement gaps, the standard of instruction in public and private schools, the effects of laws like the Right to Education Act and the Sarva Shiksha Abhiyan, and the function of the private sector. We also look at the issues that the Indian education system faces, such as a shortage of resources and educated teachers, high dropout rates, inadequate facilities, and gender and socioeconomic imbalances. Additionally, we contrast the Indian education system with that of other nations, including the American, British, Australian, and German education systems, showing the global best practices that can be adopted in India.

We've gathered facts and data from a range of sources, including official documents and reports, research studies on education, and discussions with education specialists. This information has been examined so that we can present a thorough analysis of the Indian educational system and all of its varied parts.

Educators, policymakers, students, parents, researchers, and anybody else interested in learning about the current status of education in India and the steps that may be done to improve it are among the target readers of this book.

We think that this book will be an invaluable tool for anyone trying to understand the problems with and opportunities for reform in the Indian educational system. We hope that it will spur discussion and action to ensure that every kid in India receives a quality education.

We are confident that this book will provide a comprehensive report card of Indian education system, highlighting the areas where the system is excelling, and the areas where it needs to improve.

Acknowledgements

"A Report Card" would not have been possible without the support and contributions of many individuals and organizations. We would like to extend our deepest gratitude to all those who have helped us in this journey of writing this book.

Firstly, we would like to thank the Government of India and its various educational bodies, such as the Ministry of Human Resource Development and the National Council of Educational Research and Training, for providing us with the data and information that forms the basis of this book.

We would also like to thank the private organizations and educational institutions that have provided us with valuable insights and perspectives on the Indian education system.

We would like to express our appreciation to the researchers, experts and scholars in the field of education who have shared their knowledge and expertise with us. We would like to thank the educators who have shared their experiences and perspectives on the state of education in India.

We would like to thank the publisher for providing us with the platform to share our work and for their support throughout the publishing process.

Finally, we would like to extend our appreciation to the readers of this book, for their interest and support in the Indian education system. We hope that this book has provided valuable insights and knowledge and will inspire dialogue and action towards ensuring that every child in India receives a quality education.

Historical Background Of Education In India

The history of education in India dates back to ancient times, with evidence of formal education systems in various ancient civilizations such as the Indus Valley Civilization and the Gupta Empire. Traditional Indian education, also known as Gurukul system, was centered around the guru-shishya (teacher-student) relationship, where students lived with their teachers and received a well-rounded education that included both academic and practical training.

During the colonial period, British rule introduced Western-style education in India. The British established schools and universities to educate a small elite group of Indians, primarily for administrative purposes. This led to a divide in the education system, with a small proportion of the population receiving a Western-style education while the majority continued to receive traditional Indian education.

After India gained independence in 1947, the government made significant efforts to improve and expand education in the country. In 1948, the government adopted the Universal Declaration of Human Rights, which recognized education as a basic right. The government also implemented policies aimed at increasing enrollment and improving the quality of education, such as the National Policy on Education in 1968 and the Right of Children to Free and Compulsory Education Act in 2009.

In recent years, the Indian government has implemented several policies and schemes aimed at improving education in the country, such as the Sarva Shiksha Abhiyan and the Rashtriya Madhyamik Shiksha Abhiyan. These schemes aim to increase access to education and improve the quality of education for all students, particularly for those from marginalized communities.

The Indian education system has also undergone significant changes in terms of curriculum, teaching methodologies, teacher training and assessment. The National Curriculum Framework

2005, introduced a new approach to teaching which is more student-centric and focuses on the overall development of the child. The government has also initiated several programs to improve the quality of teacher education and training.

In addition to government efforts, the private sector has also played a significant role in education in India. Private schools and colleges have grown in number, and many of them provide quality education. However, there are also concerns about the commercialization of education and the lack of regulation and oversight in the private education sector.

Overall, the history of education in India has been marked by significant changes and challenges, but also by progress and potential for further improvement. The government and private sector both have important roles to play in addressing the challenges and working towards a more inclusive and high-quality education system for all students in India.

Overview Of The Indian Education System

The Indian education system is a complex and diverse system that includes both government-run and private schools, as well as universities and colleges. The system is divided into primary, secondary, and higher education.

Primary education in India is for children between the ages of 6 and 14 and is provided by government-run schools, as well as private and international schools. Secondary education is for students between the ages of 14 and 18 and is provided by high schools and junior colleges. Higher education is provided by universities and colleges and includes undergraduate, graduate, and postgraduate programs.

The Indian government has made efforts to improve education in the country, including the implementation of the Right to Education Act in 2010, which makes education a fundamental right for children between the ages of 6 and 14. However, despite these efforts, there are still significant challenges facing the Indian education system.

One major challenge is the quality of education. In many government-run schools, there is a lack of resources and trained teachers, which can negatively impact the quality of education that students receive. Additionally, there is a significant dropout rate at the primary and secondary level, particularly among girls and children from marginalized communities.

Another challenge facing the Indian education system is the lack of access to education for certain groups of people, such as those living in rural areas or from lower socioeconomic backgrounds. This can lead to disparities in education outcomes and opportunities for different groups of people.

Despite these challenges, there is also a lot of positive progress and potential for improvement in the Indian education system. For example, the Indian government has implemented several policies and schemes, such as Sarva Shiksha Abhiyan and Rashtriya

Madhyamik Shiksha Abhiyan, aimed at improving access to education and the quality of education for all students. Additionally, the private sector has played a significant role in education in India, and there are many private schools and colleges that provide quality education.

In recent years, the Indian government has also introduced several new policies and schemes such as National Education Policy 2020, which aims to revamp the education system in India to make it more inclusive and student-centric. The policy aims to increase the literacy rate, improve the quality of education, and make education accessible to all.

Overall, the Indian education system is a complex and diverse system that faces many challenges, but also has the potential for significant improvement. The government and private sector both have important roles to play in addressing these challenges and working towards a more inclusive and high-quality education system for all students in India.

CHAPTER ONE

Present Scenario

Literacy rate and enrolment in primary, secondary and higher education

The literacy rate in India is roughly 74%, which is a strong indicator of how efficiently a nation's educational system is working. This average rate, nevertheless, conceals major differences between states and socioeconomic classes. For instance, there are large differences in literacy rates between states, and rural and urban areas have lower literacy rates than each other. States like Bihar and Arunachal Pradesh have literacy rates below 75%, whereas states like Kerala, Lakshadweep, Mizoram, and Tripura have literacy rates exceeding 90%.

Enrollment in primary education in India is relatively high, with around 96% of children of primary school age enrolled in school. However, there are still significant disparities in enrollment between different states and socioeconomic groups. For example, enrollment in rural areas is lower than in urban areas, and there are also significant disparities in enrollment between different states.

Around 75% of students participate in secondary school, which is lower than primary enrollment and is a cause for worry because it restricts the students' possibilities for post-secondary education and employment opportunities.

In comparison to other nations, India's higher education enrollment rate, which is roughly 26 percent, is very low. A rise in higher education enrollment, notably at private institutions, has, however, been observed in recent years. The increase of private colleges and universities, as well as government initiatives to broaden access to higher education, have been the main drivers of this trend.

There are also significant disparities in enrollment in higher education between different states and socioeconomic groups. For example, enrollment in higher education is lower in rural areas and among certain marginalized communities. Additionally, enrollment in certain fields of study, such as engineering and technology, is higher than in others, such as humanities and social sciences.

Overall, while the literacy rate and enrollment in primary education in India are relatively high, there are still significant disparities between different states and socioeconomic groups, and enrollment in secondary and higher education is relatively low. The government and private sector both have important roles to play in addressing these disparities and working towards increasing enrollment and literacy rates in all levels of education in India.

Disparities in education access and outcomes

Disparities in education access and outcomes are a major challenge facing the Indian education system. These disparities exist between different states, socioeconomic groups, and marginalized communities, such as Scheduled Castes and Scheduled Tribes.

One major area of disparity is in access to education. For example, access to education is lower in rural areas than in urban areas. This is due to a lack of infrastructure and resources in rural schools, as well as a lack of trained teachers. Additionally, children from lower socioeconomic backgrounds are less likely to attend school than those from higher socioeconomic backgrounds. This is due to a variety of factors, such as poverty and a lack of awareness about the importance of education.

Another area of disparity is in education outcomes. Children from marginalized communities, such as Scheduled Castes and Scheduled Tribes, are less likely to complete primary and secondary education and are also less likely to enroll in higher education. Additionally, girls are less likely to attend school and complete their education than boys, particularly in rural and marginalized communities.

These disparities in education access and outcomes can have significant long-term effects on individuals and communities. For example, individuals with less education are more likely to be unemployed or to have low-paying jobs. This can perpetuate cycles of poverty and marginalization. Additionally, communities with lower levels of education are less likely to have access to healthcare and other services, which can have negative effects on overall health and well-being.

The Indian government has implemented several policies and schemes aimed at addressing these disparities in education access and outcomes, such as Sarva Shiksha Abhiyan and Rashtriya Madhyamik Shiksha Abhiyan. These schemes aim to increase access to education and improve the quality of education for all students, particularly for those from marginalized communities.

Additionally, there are several non-government organizations and civil society groups working to address these disparities through various programs such as providing education to children from underprivileged communities, providing scholarships, creating awareness about the importance of education, and more.

Despite of these efforts, the disparities in education access and outcomes remain a significant challenge in India. Addressing these disparities requires a multifaceted approach that involves the government, private sector, and civil society working together to improve access to education and the quality of education for all students, particularly for those from marginalized communities.

Quality of education in government and private schools

The quality of education in government and private schools in India is an important issue that has a significant impact on the overall effectiveness of the country's education system.

The quality of education in government schools varies widely across the country. In many government schools, there is a lack of resources, such as textbooks, and a shortage of trained teachers. This can negatively impact the quality of education that students receive. Additionally, the infrastructure in many government schools is inadequate and not conducive to learning. This can make it difficult for students to learn and for teachers to teach effectively.

Furthermore, the quality of education in government schools is often not up to par with that of private schools. Government schools often lack the resources and facilities that private schools have, such as computer and science labs, libraries, and sports facilities. This can make it difficult for government schools to provide a well-rounded education that prepares students for the future.

On the other hand, private schools in India generally provide a higher quality of education than government schools. Private schools often have better resources, such as textbooks and technology, and a higher proportion of trained teachers. Additionally, private schools often have better facilities, such as libraries and sports facilities, which can provide students with a more well-rounded education.

However, the quality of education in private schools also varies widely, some private schools provide quality education while others may focus more on making a profit. Additionally, private schools are not accessible to many students from low-income families, thereby increasing the disparities in education access and outcomes.

The Indian government has implemented several policies and schemes aimed at improving the quality of education in government schools, such as the Sarva Shiksha Abhiyan and the Rashtriya Madhyamik Shiksha Abhiyan. These schemes aim to increase access to education and improve the quality of education for all students, particularly for those from marginalized communities.

However, despite these efforts, the quality of education in government schools remains a significant challenge in India. Addressing this challenge requires a multifaceted approach that involves the government, private sector, and civil society working together to improve the quality of education in government schools and make education accessible to all students, particularly those from marginalized communities.

CHAPTER TWO

Government Policies and Schemes

Right to Education Act

The Right of Children to Free and Compulsory Education Act, also known as the Right to Education (RTE) Act, is a law passed in India in 2009 that makes education a fundamental right for children between the ages of 6 and 14. The act applies to all schools, including government, private, and unaided schools.

The RTE Act was passed in order to address the lack of access to education for certain groups of children in India, such as those from marginalized communities or from low-income families. The act provides for several provisions to ensure that all children have access to education, such as:

Free education: All schools are required to admit children belonging to economically and socially disadvantaged groups and provide free education to them until the completion of elementary education.

No discrimination: Schools are prohibited from denying admission to children on the grounds of religion, race, caste, or socio-economic status.

Reservation: Schools are required to reserve a certain percentage of seats for children from economically and socially disadvantaged groups.

Infrastructure: Schools are required to provide infrastructure and facilities that are adequate for providing education to all children.

Teacher-student ratio: Schools are required to maintain a specific teacher-student ratio in order to ensure that children receive a quality education.

Teacher training: Teachers are required to have a certain level of qualifications and training in order to be able to teach in schools.

The RTE Act has been implemented in most of the states in India and it has been a significant step towards universalizing elementary education and towards achieving the goal of 'Education for All'.

Despite of its good intentions, the act has faced several challenges in its implementation. For example, there is a shortage of trained teachers and adequate infrastructure in many schools, which makes it difficult for schools to comply with the provisions of the act. Additionally, there have been concerns about the quality of education provided in schools, particularly in government schools.

Overall, the RTE Act is a significant step towards ensuring that all children in India have access to education, but there is still much work to be done in order to fully implement and realize the goals of the act. Addressing these challenges requires a multifaceted approach that involves the government, private sector, and civil society working together to improve the quality of education and make education accessible to all children in India.

Sarva Shiksha Abhiyan

Sarva Shiksha Abhiyan (SSA) is a flagship program of the Government of India launched in 2001, aimed at the universalization of elementary education in India. The program is implemented by the Ministry of Human Resource Development, and is managed by the Department of School Education and Literacy.

The main objective of SSA is to provide quality and inclusive education to all children in the age group of 6-14 years, by increasing access to education and improving the quality of education in government schools. The program focuses on several key areas, such as:

- Access to education: SSA aims to increase access to education for children from marginalized communities, such as Scheduled Castes, Scheduled Tribes, and children from other economically and socially disadvantaged groups.

- Quality of education: SSA aims to improve the quality of education in government schools by providing training and support to teachers and by providing resources such as textbooks, uniforms, and infrastructure.

- Inclusive education: SSA aims to provide inclusive education for children with special needs, such as children with disabilities, by providing them with special education, support and facilities.

- Gender equity: SSA aims to promote gender equity in education by providing special incentives to retain girl students and to improve their enrollment and retention rate.

- Community participation: SSA aims to involve the community in the education process by encouraging the formation of School Management Committees (SMCs) and involving parents and community members in the decision-making and monitoring process.

SSA also focuses on teacher training, as teachers are considered as the backbone of the education system. The program aims to improve the quality of teachers by providing regular training, in-service training, and provision of necessary teaching-learning materials.

Since its launch, SSA has made significant progress in increasing access to education and improving the quality.

Rashtriya Madhyamik Shiksha Abhiyan

Rashtriya Madhyamik Shiksha Abhiyan (RMSA) is a flagship program of the Government of India launched in 2009, aimed at the universalization of secondary education in India. The program is implemented by the Ministry of Human Resource Development, and is managed by the Department of School Education and Literacy.

The main objective of RMSA is to improve access to and the quality of secondary education in the country. The program focuses on several key areas, such as:

Access to education: RMSA aims to increase access to secondary education for children from marginalized communities, such as Scheduled Castes, Scheduled Tribes, and children from other economically and socially disadvantaged groups.

Quality of education: RMSA aims to improve the quality of education in government schools by providing training and support to teachers, providing resources such as textbooks, laboratory equipment and infrastructure development.

Inclusive education: RMSA aims to provide inclusive education for children with special needs, such as children with disabilities, by providing them with special education, support and facilities.

Gender equity: RMSA aims to promote gender equity in education by providing special incentives to retain girl students and to improve their enrollment and retention rate.

Community participation: RMSA aims to involve the community in the education process by encouraging the formation of School Management Committees (SMCs) and involving parents and community members in the decision-making and monitoring process.

The program also focuses on teacher training, as teachers are considered as the backbone of the education system. The program aims to improve the quality of education in India by a great extent.

National Policy on Education(NPE)

The National Policy on Education (NPE) is a policy document that lays out the framework for the development of education in India. The policy is reviewed and updated by the Government of India from time to time to keep pace with the changing needs of the education system. The most recent version of the policy was adopted in 1986 and reviewed in 1992 and 2020.

The NPE is a comprehensive policy that covers all aspects of education, including primary, secondary, higher, and technical education. It lays out the vision, goals, and objectives of the education system, and provides a framework for the development of education in the country.

One of the main goals of the NPE is to provide universal access to education for all children in India. The policy calls for the universalization of primary education, and for the provision of free and compulsory education for all children between the ages of 6 and 14. The policy also calls for the expansion of secondary and higher education to provide more opportunities for students to continue their education and to meet the needs of a growing economy.

Another important goal of the NPE is to improve the quality of education in India. The policy calls for the improvement of teacher education, the development of a more relevant curriculum, and the use of new technologies to improve the delivery of education. The policy also calls for the expansion of research and development in the field of education to improve the overall quality of the education system.

The NPE also focuses on providing inclusive education for all children, including children from marginalized communities, children with disabilities, and girls. The policy calls for the provision of special education and support for these children and for the promotion of gender equity in education.

The NPE also lays out the role of the government, private sector, and civil society in the development of education in India. The policy calls for the government to provide leadership and resources for the development of education, for the private sector to play a role in the financing and delivery of education, and for civil society to be involved in the monitoring and evaluation of the education system.

The National Policy on Education is a comprehensive policy document that provides a framework for the development of education in India. It lays out the goals, objectives and strategies for the development of education in the country. The policy is reviewed and updated by the Government of India from time to time to keep pace with the changing needs of the education system.

CHAPTER THREE

Challenges Faced by the Indian Education System

Lack of resources and trained teachers

Lack of resources and trained teachers is a major challenge facing the Indian education system. It is an issue that affects both government and private schools, and can have significant negative effects on the quality of education that students receive.

One major area of concern is the lack of resources in schools. This includes a lack of textbooks, laboratory equipment, and other learning materials. This can make it difficult for teachers to provide a quality education to their students, and can also make it difficult for students to learn effectively.

Another major area of concern is the shortage of trained teachers. Many schools, particularly in rural and under-served areas, struggle to attract and retain qualified teachers. This can result in a high proportion of untrained teachers in these schools, which can negatively impact the quality of education that students receive. Additionally, the majority of teachers in India are not trained in pedagogy, which results in a lack of teaching skills.

The shortage of resources and trained teachers is particularly acute in government schools. Government schools often lack the resources and facilities that private schools have, such as computer and science labs, libraries, and sports facilities. This can make it difficult for government schools to provide a well-rounded education that prepares students for the future.

The shortage of resources and trained teachers is a significant challenge in India, and addressing this challenge requires a multifaceted approach that involves the government, private sector, and civil society working together to improve the quality of education and make education accessible to all students, particularly those from marginalized communities.

The government has implemented several policies and schemes aimed at addressing these challenges, such as the Sarva Shiksha Abhiyan and the Rashtriya Madhyamik Shiksha Abhiyan, which aims to improve access to education and the quality of education for all students, particularly for those from marginalized communities. Additionally, the government has also implemented teacher training programs, to improve the teaching skills of the teachers.

Still the shortage of resources and trained teachers remains a significant challenge in India. Addressing this challenge requires a sustained effort over time and the participation of all stakeholders, including government, private sector, and civil society, to improve the quality of education and make education accessible to all students, particularly those from marginalized communities.

High dropout rate

The high dropout rate is a major challenge facing the Indian education system. It refers to the number of students who leave school before completing their education. The dropout rate is particularly high among children from marginalized communities, such as Scheduled Castes and Scheduled Tribes, and children from low-income families.

There are several factors that contribute to the high dropout rate in India. One of the main factors is poverty. Many children from low-income families are forced to drop out of school in order to work and support their families. Additionally, parents may not see the value of education and may not understand the importance of their children completing their education.

Another factor that contributes to the high dropout rate is the lack of access to quality education. In many rural and under-served areas, schools may lack resources, such as textbooks, and may have a shortage of trained teachers. This can make it difficult for students to learn effectively and can lead to a high dropout rate.

Additionally, the high dropout rate also reflects a lack of relevance in the education system, students may not see the relevance of what they are learning to their future aspirations, leading to a disinterest in continuing their education.

The high dropout rate also has significant long-term effects on individuals and communities. Children who drop out of school are less likely to be employed or to have well-paying jobs, which can perpetuate cycles of poverty and marginalization. Additionally, communities with high dropout rates are less likely to have access to healthcare and other services, which can have negative effects on overall health and well-being.

The Indian government has implemented several policies and schemes aimed at addressing the high dropout rate, such as the Sarva Shiksha Abhiyan and the Rashtriya Madhyamik Shiksha Abhiyan, which aim to increase access to education and improve the quality of education for all students, particularly for those from marginalized communities. Additionally, there are several non-government organizations and civil society groups working to address the high dropout rate through various programs such as providing education to children from underprivileged communities, providing scholarships, creating awareness about the importance of education, and more.

Nevertheless the high dropout rate remains a significant challenge in India. Addressing this challenge requires a multifaceted approach that involves the government, private sector, and civil society working together to improve access to quality education, and making education relevant and accessible to all students, particularly those from marginalized communities.

Inadequate infrastructure

Inadequate infrastructure is a major challenge facing the Indian education system. The infrastructure in many schools, particularly in rural and under-served areas, is inadequate and not conducive to learning. This can make it difficult for students to learn and for teachers to teach effectively, and can also negatively impact the overall quality of education.

Some of the key issues related to inadequate infrastructure include:

Lack of basic facilities: Many schools in India lack basic facilities such as toilets, clean drinking water, and electricity. This can make it difficult for students to learn and for teachers to teach effectively, and can also negatively impact students‘ health and well-being.

Shortage of classrooms: Many schools in India are overcrowded, with a shortage of classrooms. This can lead to large class sizes and make it difficult for teachers to provide individualized instruction to students.

Lack of laboratory and sports facilities: Many schools in India lack laboratory and sports facilities, which can make it difficult for students to learn science and mathematics, and also hinders physical development.

Shortage of furniture: Many schools in India lack adequate furniture, such as desks and chairs, which can make it difficult for students to learn and can also negatively impact their health and well-being.

Inadequate infrastructure can have significant negative effects on the quality of education that students receive. It can make it difficult for students to learn and for teachers to teach effectively, which can lead to a high dropout rate and negatively impact students' long-term academic and economic prospects.

The Indian government has implemented several policies and schemes aimed at addressing the inadequate infrastructure, such as the Sarva Shiksha Abhiyan and the Rashtriya Madhyamik Shiksha Abhiyan, which aim to increase access to education and improve the quality of education for all students, particularly for those from marginalized communities. Additionally, there are several non-government organizations and civil society groups working to improve the infrastructure in schools through various programs such as building new classrooms, toilets, and providing laboratory and sports facilities.

However, despite these efforts, inadequate infrastructure remains a significant challenge in India. Addressing this challenge requires a sustained effort over time, and the participation of all stakeholders, including government, private sector, and civil society, to improve access to quality education and make education accessible to all students, particularly those from marginalized communities.

CHAPTER FOUR

Disrupting the Status Quo: The Role of Private Education in India

Gender and socio-economic disparities

Gender and socio-economic disparities are major challenges facing the Indian education system. These disparities refer to the unequal access to education and the unequal outcomes of education for different groups of students, based on their gender and socio-economic status.

One major area of concern is the gender gap in education. Despite progress in recent years, girls continue to face barriers to education in India, such as early marriage and pregnancy, lack of access to toilets and sanitation facilities, and discrimination and violence in schools. These barriers often lead to girls dropping out of school at a higher rate than boys.

Another major area of concern is the socio-economic gap in education. Children from marginalized communities, such as Scheduled Castes, Scheduled Tribes, and children from other economically and socially disadvantaged groups, often have limited access to quality education and face barriers to completing their education. This results in a lower enrollment and retention rate for these children, leading to a higher dropout rate.

Both gender and socio-economic disparities in education have significant negative effects on individuals and communities. Girls who drop out of school are less likely to be employed or to have well-paying jobs, which can perpetuate cycles of poverty and marginalization. Children from marginalized communities who have limited access to quality education are less likely to have the skills and knowledge they need to succeed in the workforce and to participate fully in society.

The Indian government has implemented several policies and schemes aimed at addressing these disparities, such as the Sarva Shiksha Abhiyan and the Rashtriya Madhyamik Shiksha Abhiyan, which aim to increase access to education and improve the quality of education for all students, particularly for those from marginalized communities. Additionally, there are several non-government organizations and civil society groups working to address gender and socio-economic disparities in education through various programs such as providing education to children from underprivileged communities, providing scholarships, creating awareness about the importance of education, and more.

However, despite these efforts, gender and socio-economic disparities remain significant challenges in India. Addressing these challenges requires a multifaceted approach that involves the government, private sector, and civil society working together to improve access to quality education and make education accessible to all students, particularly those from marginalized communities and girls. Furthermore, addressing the cultural and societal attitudes towards girl's education is crucial in order to bridge the gender gap in education.

Growth of private schools and colleges

The growth of private schools and colleges is a significant trend in the Indian education system. While the government has been the primary provider of education in India for many years, the number of private schools and colleges has been increasing rapidly in recent years. The growth of private education has been driven by a number of factors, including the increasing demand for education, the limited capacity of government schools and colleges, and the perceived higher quality of education offered by private institutions.

One of the key advantages of private schools is that they often offer a higher quality of education than government schools. Private schools are able to attract better-trained teachers, have access to more resources, and offer a wider range of extracurricular activities. Additionally, private schools also have more autonomy over their curriculum and pedagogy, which allows them to offer more innovative and personalized education.

The growth of private colleges has also been driven by the increasing demand for higher education in India. With a growing economy and a growing middle class, more and more students are seeking higher education, and private colleges have been able to meet this demand by offering a wide range of courses and programs. Additionally, private colleges are often able to offer more specialized and career-oriented courses than government colleges.

However, the growth of private education has also raised some concerns. Private schools and colleges can be quite expensive, which can make them inaccessible to many students from low-income families. Additionally, there are concerns about the quality of education offered by some private institutions, as well as issues of transparency and accountability.

The government has taken steps to regulate private education and ensure that private institutions are held to the same standards as government institutions. However, with the high demand for education, the growth of private schools and colleges is likely to continue in the future.

In conclusion, the growth of private schools and colleges is a significant trend in the Indian education system. While private schools and colleges have been able to meet the increasing demand for education and offer a higher quality of education than government institutions, the high cost of private education remains a concern and there are also concerns about the quality of education offered by some private institutions. The government has taken steps to regulate private education, but addressing this challenge requires a sustained effort over time, and the participation of all stakeholders, including government, private sector.

Impact of private sector on education access and quality

The impact of the private sector on education access and quality is a complex issue in the Indian education system. On one hand, the private sector has played a significant role in increasing access to education, particularly in rural and under-served areas where government schools are scarce. Additionally, private schools and colleges often provide a higher quality of education than government schools and colleges, with better facilities and resources, more experienced and qualified teachers, and more specialized and vocational programs.

On the other hand, the growth of private education has also led to certain negative consequences. Private education can be more expensive than government education, which can make it difficult for students from low-income families to afford. Additionally, private schools and colleges may have their own admission criteria and may not be accessible to all students, which can perpetuate socio-economic disparities in education.

Furthermore, the focus on profit-making in private schools and colleges can result in cut corners and compromise on the quality of education provided. Additionally, the private sector is not always held to the same standards as the government sector, which can lead to a lack of accountability and oversight.

The Indian government has implemented several policies and schemes aimed at addressing the impact of the private sector on education access and quality. The Right to Education Act guarantees every child the right to free and compulsory education, and the National Education Policy lays out the framework for the development of education in India. Additionally, there are several regulations in place to ensure the quality of education provided by private schools and colleges, such as the accreditation of schools and colleges by the National Accreditation and Assessment Council (NAAC) and the University Grants Commission (UGC).

Despite these efforts, the impact of the private sector on education access and quality remains a complex issue.

Challenges faced by the private education sector

The private education sector in India faces several challenges that affect the quality and accessibility of education for students. These challenges include:

Quality of Education: Ensuring the quality of education provided by private schools and colleges is a major challenge. Some private institutions may cut corners in order to increase profits, which can lead to a decrease in the quality of education provided. Additionally, private institutions may not be held to the same standards as government institutions, which can lead to a lack of accountability and oversight.

Affordability: Making private education affordable for students from low-income families is a significant challenge. Tuition fees in private institutions can be higher than in government institutions, which can make it difficult for students from low-income families to afford a private education.

Regulation and oversight: The private education sector is not always well-regulated, which can lead to a lack of oversight and accountability. This can result in institutions not following the rules, which can lead to a lack of quality control and lower standards.

Attracting and retaining quality teachers: Attracting and retaining quality teachers is a challenge for private schools and colleges. Private institutions may not be able to offer the same salary and benefits as government institutions, which can make it difficult to attract and retain qualified teachers.

Curriculum and Accreditation: Private institutions may not follow the same curriculum as government institutions, which can lead to a lack of standardization and uniformity in the education provided. Additionally, private institutions may not be accredited by the National Accreditation and Assessment Council (NAAC) and the University Grants Commission (UGC), which can lead to a lack of oversight and accountability.

Competition: The private education sector is highly competitive, with many institutions vying for the same students. This can lead to institutions cutting corners and compromising on the quality of education provided in order to attract more students.

To address these challenges, the Indian government has implemented various policies and regulations such as the Right to Education Act, National Education Policy and regulations of accreditation of schools and colleges by the National Accreditation and Assessment Council (NAAC) and the University Grants Commission (UGC). The government is also working with private institutions to improve the quality and accessibility of education for students. However, despite these efforts, the challenges facing the private education sector in India remain significant and addressing them requires the participation of all stakeholders, including the government, private sector and civil society.

CHAPTER FIVE

A World View: Indian Education in the Global Arena

Comparison of Indian education system with American Education System

The Indian education system and the American education system are both large and complex systems, but they have significant differences in terms of structure, funding, and curriculum.

One of the main differences between the two systems is the structure of the education system. The American education system is divided into three levels: primary, secondary, and post-secondary education. The primary and secondary levels are also known as K-12 education. The Indian education system is also divided into three levels: primary, secondary, and higher education. However, the structure of the Indian education system is more complex than the American education system. The Indian education system also has different levels of education such as pre-primary, upper primary, and lower secondary education. Additionally, the Indian education system also has a vocational education system for students who want to pursue non-academic careers.

Another key difference is the funding of the education systems. The American education system is mainly funded by the government, state and local authorities. The government provides funding to public schools through the Elementary and Secondary Education Act (ESEA) and the Higher Education Act (HEA). Private schools, on the other hand, are mostly funded by tuition fees, donations, and other private sources. In contrast, the Indian education system is mainly funded by the government, but also receives funding from private sources and tuition fees. However, the funding for the Indian education system is not as consistent as the American education system, leading to disparities in education access and outcomes.

The curriculum is also different between the two systems. The American education system follows a standardized curriculum set by the government, but individual states have some flexibility to adapt the curriculum to their needs. The Indian education system follows a centralized curriculum set by the government, but individual states and schools also have some flexibility to adapt the curriculum to their needs. Furthermore, the American education system places more emphasis on critical thinking and problem-solving skills, while the Indian education system places more emphasis on rote learning and memorization.

In terms of student outcomes, the American education system has a higher literacy rate and enrollment in primary, secondary and higher education compared to the Indian education system. Additionally, American students tend to score higher on international test such as PISA and TIMSS. However, the American education system also faces challenges such as a significant achievement gap between different socio-economic groups and ethnicities.

In conclusion, the Indian education system and the American education system have significant differences in terms of structure, funding, curriculum, and student outcomes. Both systems have their own strengths and challenges, and they can learn from each other. However, it's important to note that the comparison of education system is complex, and it's not possible to generalize the entire system based on a few points.

Comparison of Indian education system with UK Education System

The Indian education system and the UK education system are both large and complex systems, but they have significant differences in terms of structure, funding, and curriculum.

One of the main differences between the two systems is the structure of the education system. The UK education system is divided into four levels: primary, secondary, further education, and higher education. The Indian education system is also divided into three levels: primary, secondary, and higher education. However, the structure of the Indian education system is more complex than the UK education system. The Indian education system also has different levels of education such as pre-primary, upper primary, and lower secondary education. Additionally, the Indian education system also has a vocational education system for students who want to pursue non-academic careers.

Another key difference is the funding of the education systems. The UK education system is mainly funded by the government through the Department for Education. The government provides funding to public schools and also provides financial aid for students from low-income families to attend private schools or universities. In contrast, the Indian education system is mainly funded by the government, but also receives funding from private sources and tuition fees. However, the funding for the Indian education system is not as consistent as the UK education system, leading to disparities in education access and outcomes.

The curriculum is also different between the two systems. The UK education system follows a standardized curriculum set by the government, but individual schools have some flexibility to adapt the curriculum to their needs. The Indian education system follows a centralized curriculum set by the government, but individual states and schools also have some flexibility to adapt the curriculum to their needs. Furthermore, the UK education system places more emphasis on critical thinking and problem-solving skills, while the Indian education system places more emphasis on rote learning and memorization.

In terms of student outcomes, the UK education system has a higher literacy rate and enrollment in primary, secondary and higher education compared to the Indian education system. Additionally, UK students tend to score higher on international test such as PISA and TIMSS. However, the UK education system also faces challenges such as a significant achievement gap between different socio-economic groups and ethnicities.

In conclusion, the Indian education system and the UK education system have significant differences in terms of structure, funding, curriculum, and student outcomes. Both systems have their own strengths and challenges, and they can learn from each other. However, it's important to note that the comparison of education system is complex, and it's not possible to generalize the entire system based on a few points. Additionally, cultural and societal factors of both countries also play an important role in shaping the education system.

Comparison of Indian education system with Australian Education System

The Indian education system and the Australian education system are both large and complex systems, but they have significant differences in terms of structure, funding, and curriculum.

One of the main differences between the two systems is the structure of the education system. The Australian education system is divided into three levels: primary, secondary, and tertiary education. The Indian education system is also divided into three levels: primary, secondary, and higher education. However, the structure of the Indian education system is more complex than the Australian education system. The Indian education system also has different levels of education such as pre-primary, upper primary, and lower secondary education. Additionally, the Indian education system also has a vocational education system for students who want to pursue non-academic careers.

Another key difference is the funding of the education systems. The Australian education system is mainly funded by the government through the Department of Education. The government provides funding to public schools and also provides financial aid for students from low-income families to attend private schools or universities. In contrast, the Indian education system is mainly funded by the government, but also receives funding from private sources and tuition fees. However, the funding for the Indian education system is not as consistent as the Australian education system, leading to disparities in education access and outcomes.

The curriculum is also different between the two systems. The Australian education system follows a standardized curriculum set by the government, but individual states have some flexibility to adapt the curriculum to their needs. The Indian education system follows a centralized curriculum set by the government, but individual states and schools also have some flexibility to adapt the curriculum to their needs. Furthermore, the Australian education system places more emphasis on critical thinking and problem-solving skills, while the Indian education system places more emphasis on rote learning and memorization.

In terms of student outcomes, the Australian education system has a higher literacy rate and enrollment in primary, secondary and higher education compared to the Indian education system. Additionally, Australian students tend to score higher on international test such as PISA and TIMSS. However, the Australian education system also faces challenges such as a significant achievement gap between different socio-economic groups and ethnicities.

In conclusion, the Indian education system and the Australian education system have significant differences in terms of structure, funding, curriculum, and student outcomes. Both systems have their own strengths and challenges, and they can learn from each other. However, it's important to note that the comparison of education system is complex, and it's not possible to generalize the entire system based on a few points. Additionally, cultural and societal factors of both countries also play an important role in shaping the education system.

Comparison of Indian education system with German Education System

The Indian education system and the German education system are both large and complex systems, but they have significant differences in terms of structure, funding, and curriculum.

One of the main differences between the two systems is the structure of the education system. The German education system is divided into four levels: primary, lower secondary, upper secondary and higher education. The Indian education system is also divided into three levels: primary, secondary, and higher education. However, the structure of the Indian education system is more complex than the German education system. The Indian education system also has different levels of education such as pre-primary, upper primary, and lower secondary education. Additionally, the Indian education system also has a vocational education system for students who want to pursue non-academic careers.

Another key difference is the funding of the education systems. The German education system is mainly funded by the government and the states. The government provides funding to public schools and also provides financial aid for students from low-income families to attend private schools or universities. In contrast, the Indian education system is mainly funded by the government, but also receives funding from private sources and tuition fees. However, the funding for the Indian education system is not as consistent as the German education system, leading to disparities in education access and outcomes.

The curriculum is also different between the two systems. The German education system follows a standardized curriculum set by the government, but individual states have some flexibility to adapt the curriculum to their needs. The Indian education system follows a centralized curriculum set by the government, but individual states and schools also have some flexibility to adapt the curriculum to their needs. Furthermore, the German education system places more emphasis on practical and vocational training, while the Indian education system places more emphasis on rote learning and memorization.

In terms of student outcomes, the German education system has a high literacy rate and enrollment in primary, secondary and higher education compared to the Indian education system. Additionally, German students tend to score higher on international test such as PISA and TIMSS. German education system is known for its strong emphasis on vocational education which gives students the opportunity to gain practical skills and knowledge, and enter the workforce with a solid skill set. However, the German education system also faces challenges such as a significant achievement gap between different socio-economic groups and ethnic communities.

More on German Education System –

The German education system is known for its strong emphasis on vocational education and its dual system of education which combines theoretical and practical training. This system is designed to provide students with the skills and knowledge needed to enter the workforce immediately after completing their education.

The German vocational education system is divided into three levels: basic vocational training, advanced vocational training, and vocational training in a higher education context. Basic vocational training is usually completed in two years, and students can then proceed to advanced vocational training which usually takes another two years. After completing advanced vocational training, students can choose to pursue vocational training in a higher education context which can lead to a bachelor's degree. This system provides students with a clear pathway to enter the workforce or to pursue further education.

Another key feature of the German education system is the emphasis on continuous assessment and evaluations throughout the students' education. This allows teachers to track student progress and identify any areas where students may need additional support. The German education system also places a strong emphasis on teamwork and projects, which allows students to develop important skills such as problem-solving, critical thinking, and communication.

The German education system is also known for its high-quality teachers and well-equipped schools. Teachers in Germany are required to have a teaching degree, and they are well-trained and well-compensated. Additionally, schools in Germany are well-equipped with modern technology and resources to support student learning.

However, the German education system also faces certain challenges. One of the main challenges is the significant achievement gap between different socio-economic groups and ethnicities. Additionally, the German education system has been criticized for not providing students with enough flexibility to choose their own career paths.

In conclusion, the German education system is known for its strong emphasis on vocational education and its dual system of education which combines theoretical and practical training. This system provides students with the skills and knowledge needed to enter the workforce immediately after completing their education. The German education system is also known for its high-quality teachers and well-equipped schools.

Comparison of Indian education system with Canadian Education System

The Indian education system and the Canadian education system are both large and complex systems, but they have significant differences in terms of structure, funding, and curriculum.

One of the main differences between the two systems is the structure of the education system. The Canadian education system is divided into three levels: primary, secondary, and post-secondary education. The Indian education system is also divided into three levels: primary, secondary, and higher education. However, the structure of the Indian education system is more complex than the Canadian education system. The Indian education system also has different levels of education such as pre-primary, upper primary, and lower secondary education. Additionally, the Indian education system also has a vocational education system for students who want to pursue non-academic careers.

Another key difference is the funding of the education systems. The Canadian education system is mainly funded by the government through the Ministry of Education. The government provides funding to public schools and also provides financial aid for students from low-income families to attend private schools or universities. In contrast, the Indian education system is mainly funded by the government, but also receives funding from private sources and tuition fees. However, the funding for the Indian education system is not as consistent as the Canadian education system, leading to disparities in education access and outcomes.

The curriculum is also different between the two systems. The Canadian education system follows a standardized curriculum set by the government, but individual provinces have some flexibility to adapt the curriculum to their needs. The Indian education system follows a centralized curriculum set by the government, but individual states and schools also have some flexibility to adapt the curriculum to their needs. Furthermore, the Canadian education system places more emphasis on critical thinking and problem-solving skills, while the Indian education system places more emphasis on rote learning and memorization.

In terms of student outcomes, the Canadian education system has a high literacy rate and enrollment in primary, secondary and higher education compared to the Indian education system. Additionally, Canadian students tend to score higher on international test such as PISA and TIMSS. However, the Canadian education system also faces challenges such as a significant achievement gap between different socio-economic groups and ethnicities.

The Canadian education system also places a heavy emphasis on inclusion and diversity, with policies and programs in place to support students from different backgrounds and abilities. This includes support for indigenous students, language and cultural programs for immigrant students, and special education programs for students with disabilities.

Another key feature of the Canadian education system is the emphasis on co-op and internship programs, which allow students to gain practical experience and make connections in their field.

International best practices and implications for India

The Indian education system, like many other education systems around the world, faces a number of challenges. These challenges include low literacy rates, high dropout rates, inadequate infrastructure, disparities in education access and outcomes, lack of resources and trained teachers, and gender and socio-economic disparities. To address these challenges, it is important to look at international best practices and consider their implications for the Indian education system.

One international best practice that has been successful in improving education outcomes is the emphasis on early childhood education. Studies have shown that investing in early childhood education can lead to better academic performance, improved social skills, and a higher likelihood of graduating from high school. Additionally, providing access to quality early childhood education can also help to reduce disparities in education access and outcomes. This can be achieved by investing in pre-primary education and providing universal access to quality education for children aged 3-6 years.

Another international best practice that has been successful in improving education outcomes is the use of data and technology in education. This includes using data to track student progress, identify areas for improvement, and target resources where they are needed most. Additionally, technology can be used to support student learning, such as through online learning platforms and virtual classrooms. This can be implemented by incorporating digital education and e-learning in the curriculum and providing access to technology and internet in schools.

In terms of teacher training and development, best practices include providing ongoing professional development opportunities and implementing performance-based evaluations. This can help to ensure that teachers are well-trained and equipped to support student learning. Furthermore, providing teachers with the necessary resources, technology, and support can help them to deliver high-quality instruction. This can be achieved by providing in-service training, continuous professional development and performance-based evaluations for teachers.

In order to improve education outcomes, it is also important to address socio-economic and cultural disparities. This includes providing support and resources to disadvantaged students, such as students from low-income families, rural areas, and minority groups. Additionally, providing support for students with special needs and disabilities is also crucial. This can be achieved by providing inclusive education and special education programs, and also providing financial aid and scholarships for students from marginalized communities.

Another international best practice is the use of innovative teaching methods and curriculum that support student-centered learning. This includes methods such as project-based learning, problem-based learning, and inquiry-based learning. These methods encourage students to think critically and independently, and to take an active role in their own learning.

Exploring the Challenges and Opportunities in India's Education System

India's education system has come a long way in the past few decades. However, as the world becomes increasingly globalized, it is important to examine how India's education system compares to the best in the world.

One of the key areas where India falls behind is in terms of literacy rates. According to UNESCO, India's literacy rate in 2018 was 74.04%. This is lower than many developed nations such as Japan (99%), South Korea (97.9%), and Canada (97.7%).

In terms of primary education, India has made significant progress in increasing enrollment and reducing dropout rates. The Gross Enrollment Ratio (GER) in primary education in India was 96.7% in 2019-2020 and the dropout rate at the primary level was 7.4% in 2019-2020. However, the GER in secondary education is much lower at 69.7%, indicating that there is still a significant gap in enrollment between primary and secondary education in India.

The quality of education in India is also an area of concern. According to the National Achievement Survey (NAS), the average percentage of students who score above 50% in Class X and XII board exams is around 60%. This indicates that there is a significant percentage of students who are not performing well academically. Additionally, the National Institution Ranking Framework (NIRF) 2021 shows that Indian higher education institutions are not yet at par with the best in the world.

Another area where India falls behind is in terms of access to technology and internet in education. According to the National Sample Survey Office (NSSO), the percentage of households with access to the internet in India was 27% in 2019. This highlights the digital divide in India and the need for greater access to technology and internet in schools.

In terms of teacher training and professional development, India also lags behind other countries. According to a report by the National Council of Educational Research and Training (NCERT), the number of trained teachers in primary and secondary schools in India is only 66%. This highlights the need for more investment in teacher training and professional development.

Despite these challenges, India has made significant progress in increasing enrollment and literacy rates, and the government has implemented policies such as the Right to Education (RTE) Act and Sarva Shiksha Abhiyan (SSA) to improve access to education. Additionally, the growth of private schools in India has provided more options for students and families.

CHAPTER SIX

Why do Indian students go abroad for their higher education?

Indian students have been increasingly going abroad for their higher education in recent years. There are several reasons for this trend, including the perceived lack of quality in the Indian education system, the limited number of seats available in top-ranked universities in India, the desire to study in a global environment and acquire international exposure, and the lack of specific programs or specializations offered in India.

One of the main reasons why Indian students go abroad for higher education is the perceived lack of quality in the Indian education system. The Indian education system has been criticized for its focus on rote learning and memorization, lack of emphasis on critical thinking and problem-solving skills, and inadequate infrastructure and resources. Additionally, there is a shortage of well-trained and qualified teachers in the Indian education system. Many Indian students believe that the quality of education offered in foreign universities is superior to that offered in India, and that studying abroad will give them better opportunities to develop the skills and knowledge they need to succeed in their chosen field.

Another reason why Indian students go abroad for higher education is the limited number of seats available in top-ranked universities in India. The demand for higher education in India is high, but the supply of seats in top-ranked universities is limited. This has led many Indian students to look for higher education opportunities abroad, where there is a larger number of seats available in top-ranked universities.

The desire to study in a global environment and acquire international exposure is another reason why Indian students go abroad for higher education. Studying abroad exposes students to different cultures, languages, and ways of thinking, which can broaden their perspectives and help them to become more culturally aware and adaptable. Additionally, studying abroad can also provide students with the opportunity to make international connections and network with people from different parts of the world.

Lastly, the lack of specific programs or specializations offered in India is also a significant reason why many Indian students choose to go abroad for their higher education. For example, many Indian students go to foreign countries to pursue programs in fields such as engineering, computer science, and business, which are in high demand in the current job market. These students believe that the curriculum and the teaching methods offered in foreign universities are more advanced than those offered in India.

In conclusion, Indian students go abroad for higher education for several reasons, including the perceived lack of quality in the Indian education system, the limited number of seats available in top-ranked universities in India, the desire to study in a global environment and acquire international exposure.

CHAPTER SEVEN

CONCLUSION

Summary of key findings

The above research notes were discussing different aspects of the Indian education system, including the historical background, literacy rate and enrollment, disparities in education access and outcomes, quality of education in government and private schools, Right to Education Act, Sarva Shiksha Abhiyan, Rashtriya Madhyamik Shiksha Abhiyan, National Policy on Education, lack of resources and trained teachers, high dropout rate, inadequate infrastructure, Gender and socio-economic disparities, growth of private schools and colleges, impact of private sector on education access and quality, challenges facing the private education sector, and a comparison of the Indian education system with various other countries education systems (American, UK, Australian, German and Canadian education systems).

The key findings from these research notes include:

The Indian education system is complex and faces a number of challenges such as low literacy rates, high dropout rates, inadequate infrastructure, disparities in education access and outcomes, lack of resources and trained teachers, and gender and socio-economic disparities.

The Indian education system is mainly funded by the government, but also receives funding from private sources and tuition fees. However, the funding for the Indian education system is not as consistent as other countries education system, leading to disparities in education access and outcomes.

The Indian education system has been criticized for its focus on rote learning and lack of emphasis on critical thinking and problem-solving skills.

The Indian education system also has a vocational education system for students who want to pursue non-academic careers.

The Indian education system follows a centralized curriculum set by the government, but individual states and schools also have some flexibility to adapt the curriculum to their needs.

The Indian education system places more emphasis on rote learning and memorization than critical thinking and problem-solving skills.

The Indian education system also faces challenges such as a significant achievement gap between different socio-economic groups and ethnicities.

The Indian students are attracted to study in a global environment and acquire international exposure, as it helps them to broaden their perspectives and adapt to different cultures, languages and ways of thinking.

Many Indian students go abroad for higher education due to the lack of specific programs or specializations offered in India, such as engineering, computer science, and business, which are in high demand in the current job market.

Socio-economic and cultural disparities also play a role in Indian students choosing to study abroad, as many students from marginalized communities may not have access to the same quality of education or opportunities as those from more privileged backgrounds.

Suggestions for improvement

The Indian education system faces a number of challenges, including low literacy rates, high dropout rates, inadequate infrastructure, disparities in education access and outcomes, lack of resources and trained teachers, and gender and socio-economic disparities. In order to address these challenges and improve the Indian education system, a number of suggestions can be made.

One suggestion is to focus on early childhood education. Investing in early childhood education can lead to better academic performance, improved social skills, and a higher likelihood of graduating from high school. Additionally, providing access to quality early childhood education can also help to reduce disparities in education access and outcomes. This can be achieved by providing universal access to pre-primary education for children aged 3-6 years, and also by investing in infrastructure and resources for pre-primary education.

Another suggestion is to use data and technology in education. This includes using data to track student progress, identify areas for improvement, and target resources where they are needed most. Additionally, technology can be used to support student learning, such as through online learning platforms and virtual classrooms. This can be achieved by incorporating digital education and e-learning in the curriculum and providing access to technology and internet in schools.

In terms of teacher training and development, providing ongoing professional development opportunities and implementing performance-based evaluations is crucial. This can help to ensure that teachers are well-trained and equipped to support student learning. Furthermore, providing teachers with the necessary resources, technology and support can help them to deliver high-quality instruction. This can be achieved by providing in-service training, continuous professional development and performance-based evaluations for teachers.

In order to improve education outcomes, it is also important to address socio-economic and cultural disparities. This includes providing support and resources to disadvantaged students, such as students from low-income families, rural areas, and minority groups. Additionally, providing support for students with special needs and disabilities is also crucial. This can be achieved by providing inclusive education and special education programs, and also providing financial aid and scholarships for students from marginalized communities.

Another suggestion is to use innovative teaching methods and curriculum that support student-centered learning. This includes methods such as project-based learning, problem-based learning, and inquiry-based learning. These methods encourage students to think critically and independently, and to take an active role in their own learning. This can be achieved by revising the curriculum to incorporate student-centered learning methods and providing training for teachers on how to implement these methods.

Another suggestion is to increase the number of seats in top-ranked universities in India. This can be achieved by increasing the number of universities and colleges in the country, increasing the intake of students in existing universities and colleges, and also by providing financial aid and scholarships to students.

Lastly, it is important to increase the funding for the Indian education system. This can be achieved by increasing the allocation of funds for education in the national budget, and also by increasing the participation of private sector in the education system through public-private partnerships.

In conclusion, there are a number of suggestions that can be made to improve the Indian education system. These include focusing on early childhood education, using data and technology in education, providing ongoing professional development opportunities for teachers, addressing socio-economic and cultural disparities, using innovative teaching methods and curriculum, increasing the number of seats in top-ranked universities, and increasing funding for the Indian education system. These suggestions, if implemented effectively, can help to address the challenges facing the Indian education system and improve education outcomes for students.

Statistics And Data On Indian Education

According to the UNESCO Institute for Statistics, the literacy rate in India was 74.04% in 2018. While this number may seem high, it is important to note that there are significant disparities in literacy rates between different states and regions in India. For example, states such as Kerala and Goa have literacy rates of 96.2% and 88.7% respectively, while states such as Bihar and Rajasthan have literacy rates of 63.8% and 67.7% respectively.

The Gross Enrolment Ratio (GER) in primary education in India was 96.7% in 2019-2020. This means that 96.7% of children aged 6-11 were enrolled in primary education. However, the GER in secondary education was only 69.7%, indicating that there is still a significant gap in enrollment between primary and secondary education in India.

The dropout rate at the primary level in India was 7.4% in 2019-2020, while the dropout rate at the secondary level was 20.4%. The dropout rate is particularly high in certain states such as Odisha, Jharkhand and Chhattisgarh. The dropout rate is also higher for girls than boys, and for students from disadvantaged backgrounds such as those from low-income families and rural areas.

According to a report by the World Bank, India has the largest population of out-of-school children in the world, with approximately 32.8 million children aged 6-13 not attending school in 2018. This is primarily due to poverty, lack of access to schools, and social and cultural barriers.

According to the Annual Status of Education Report (ASER) 2021, the percentage of children who are not enrolled in school is highest in rural areas of India, with a rate of 8.2% as compared to urban areas where the rate is 3.3%. This highlights the disparities in education access and outcomes between rural and urban areas in India.

The ASER report also states that the percentage of children in Class III who can read a Class II level text is only 48.1%. This indicates that there are significant gaps in learning outcomes in the Indian education system.

According to the National Sample Survey Office (NSSO), the percentage of households with access to the internet in India was 27% in 2019. This highlights the digital divide in India and the need for greater access to technology and internet in schools.

According to a report by the National Council of Educational Research and Training (NCERT), the student-teacher ratio in primary schools in India is 30:1, while the student-teacher ratio in secondary schools is 35:1. This indicates that there is a shortage of teachers in the Indian education system, which can negatively impact the quality of education.

The NCERT report also states that the number of trained teachers in primary and secondary schools in India is only 66%. This highlights the need for more investment in teacher training and professional development.

India has increased from 18.9% in 2005-2006 to 27.2% in 2016-2017. While the growth of private schools in India can provide more options for students and families, it also highlights the disparities in education access and outcomes between those who can afford private education and those who cannot.

According to the National Achievement Survey (NAS), the average percentage of students who score above 50% in Class X and XII board exams is around 60%. This indicates that there is a significant percentage of students who are not performing well academically.

According to the National Institution Ranking Framework (NIRF), in 2021, Indian Institute of Technology, Madras (IIT-M) and Indian Institute of Science (IISc) are the top-ranked institutions in India. However, the overall quality and reputation of higher education institutions in India is still lower than that of institutions in developed countries.

In conclusion, while the Indian education system has made significant progress in increasing enrollment and literacy rates, there are still significant challenges in terms of quality of education, disparities in education access and outcomes, shortage of teachers, and inadequate infrastructure. To improve the Indian education system, it is important to address these challenges through targeted investments and policies. Additionally, focusing on early childhood education, using technology and data in education, addressing socio-economic and cultural disparities, and increasing funding for education are key steps that can be taken to improve the Indian education system.

Government Documents And Reports On Education In India

Over the years, the Indian government has published a variety of papers and documents available about the condition of education in India. Key government documents and reports include the following:

The government's goal for the Indian educational system is outlined in the National Policy on Education (NPE), a policy statement. It was created in 1986 and most recently revised in 2016. The policy statement discusses a number of education-related topics, such as making elementary education universal, raising the standard of education, and utilising technology in the classroom.

The Right to Education Act (RTE) The Indian government passed the Right to Education Act in 2009, ensuring free and mandatory education for kids between the ages of 6 and 14.

The statute also specifies rules for school facilities, student-to-teacher ratios, and other educational aspects.

To ensure that all children in India receive a primary education, the Indian government announced the Sarva Shiksha Abhiyan (SSA) initiative in 2001. All children between the ages of 6 and 14 are expected to receive a high-quality elementary education as part of the programme.

Rashtriya Madhyamik Shiksha Abhiyan (RMSA): The Indian government introduced Rashtriya Madhyamik Shiksha Abhiyan in 2009 to increase secondary school enrollment and raise academic standards.

The National Curriculum Framework (NCF) is a document that outlines the specifications for the curriculum in Indian schools. The last update was made in 2005.

National Achievement Survey (NAS): To evaluate the learning outcomes of children in schools everywhere throughout India, the National Council of Educational Research and Training (NCERT) conducted the National Achievement Survey.

The Annual Status of Education Report (ASER) is a census that Pratham, a non - profit organisation, performs to evaluate the educational progress of children in schools all over India.

Report on education by the National Sample Survey Office (NSSO): A survey on several areas of education in India is conducted by the National Sample Survey Office, including enrolment, literacy, & access to technology in the classroom.

National Institution Ranking Framework (NIRF): The National Institution Ranking Framework is a framework developed by the Ministry of Human Resource Development to rank higher education institutions in India.

Last Word

"*We hope that this book has provided valuable insights and knowledge into the Indian education system. From the historical background to the current challenges and solutions, we have aimed to provide a comprehensive analysis of the state of education in India. We have also highlighted the impact of the private sector and the global best practices that can be implemented in India. We have tried to cover all the aspects of Indian education system.*

We would like to extend our deepest appreciation to all the readers who have invested their time in reading this book. Your support and engagement have been invaluable in our quest for educational excellence.

This book is just a small step in the journey of Indian Education System and we believe that there is still a lot to be done in the field of education in India.

For more updates on Indian Education System and other related topics, follow the author on Instagram at @real_anuragyadav

If you have enjoyed reading this book, we would greatly appreciate it if you could leave a review on the platform where you have purchased the book.

Also, we invite you to check out other books written by the author, which cover a range of topics related to Indian education system, and we are sure you will find them informative and enlightening.

"

Thank You

Your investment in this book is an investment in the future of Indian education.

Printed by Libri Plureos GmbH in Hamburg,
Germany